How to Dazzle at

BEGINNING MAPSKILLS

Vivienne Horobin

Brilliant Publications

Other books in the series:

Published by Brilliant Publications
1 Church View,
Sparrow Hall Farm,
Edlesborough,
Dunstable,
Bedfordshire
LU6 2ES, UK

Tel: 01525 229720
Fax: 01525 229725
E-mail: sales@brilliantpublications.co.uk
Website: www.brilliantpublications.co.uk

The name Brilliant Publications and the logo are registered trademarks.

Written by Vivienne Horobin
Illustrated by Pat Murray
Cover designed and illustrated by Lynda Murray

© Vivienne Horobin 2004
ISBN 1 903853 58 3

First printed and published in the UK in 2004

Contents

Introduction

How to Dazzle at Beginning Mapskills contains 43 photocopiable sheets for use with pupils who are working at Level 3 of the National Curriculum. The material is all related to the skills element of the Programme of Study for the National Curriculum, focussing in particular on the Local Area and culminating in activities based on the British Isles, Europe and the World. The activities are presented in an age-appropriate manner and provide a flexible but structured resource for teaching pupils to develop an understanding of direction and location in relation to simple maps.

The first part of the book concentrates on routes and common locational words together with a simple explanation of compass points; this is followed by looking at the Local Area, including local buildings, people and facilities, as well as related vocabulary. There are some more advanced concepts, such as land use maps and a wind rose, which introduce secondary data. The last part uses maps of Britain, Europe and the World to introduce or develop a basic knowledge of these areas while, at the same time, reinforcing vocabulary and concepts of direction.

Map reading requires a spatial awareness that can be demanding for some pupils, but it is a useful skill to acquire and may be needed in various situations and occupations. The basic concepts are explained in a simple and gradual way and applied in various contexts designed to be interesting and enjoyable.

How to use the book

All of the activity sheets can be used separately without the need for further resources. Occasionally, more than one page is required to complete an exercise and where this is so, it is clearly indicated in the text.

The activity sheets vary a little in levels of difficulty and a teacher may not want all the pupils to complete all the activities. Some of the activities are similar, requiring the same sort of response but using a different format, and this may be helpful for reinforcing knowledge. Different activities also appeal to different children.

While there is obviously no need to use the sheets in the order they appear in the book, the skills and concepts do tend to build upon preceding activities in a sequential manner. This is to allow progression and consolidation where necessary. In addition, some activities can be used as simple tests for assessment purposes.

Most of the main activities are designed for pupils to complete individually but the Add-on exercises sometimes involve the pupils working in pairs. The Add-on exercises are all designed to encourage consolidation but may also involve simple research and application of the concept in a broader context.

Where is it?

There are many words we use to describe where people, places and things are. We use words like opposite, behind, left, right, above, when we want to explain where things are.

Make a list of words which tell you where something is:

1. _____   6. _____

2. _____   7. _____

3. _____   8. _____

4. _____   9. _____

5. _____   10. _____

Now look at the words below. With a bright colour, colour in all the shapes that contain words and phrases which help to describe where things are.

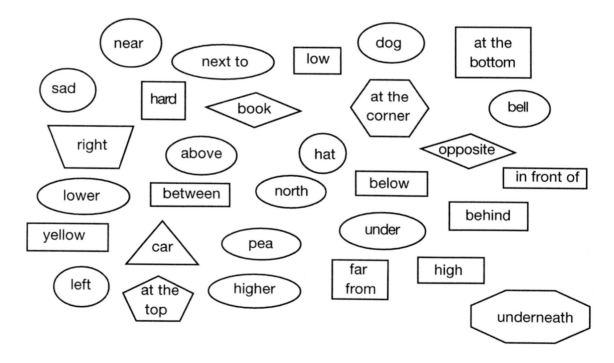

Add-on

Do this with a friend. Think of some sentences to describe the position of objects in the classroom, using some of the words on this page.

Classroom lockers - diagram

TOP

Alison o	**Amy** o	**Robert** o	**Jasmin** o
Josef o	**Ben** o	**Rashmi** o	**Jane** o
Emily o	**Paul** o	**Rosie** o	**Mark** o
Marie o	**Sajed** o	**Chloe** o	**Rachel** o

LEFT

RIGHT

BOTTOM

Where are the lockers?

Look at the diagram showing the classroom lockers.

Answer true or false to each of the following statements.

Jasmin's locker is in the top row. ....

Paul's locker is underneath Emily's. ....

Josef's locker is above Alison's. ....

Chloe's locker is below Rosie's. ....

Jane's locker is under Mark's. ....

Mark's locker is higher than Marie's. ....

Josef's locker is to the right of Ben's. ....

Paul's locker is lower than Jasmin's. ....

Ben's locker is next to Jane's. ....

Marie's locker is in the bottom row. ....

Hint

Right ⟶

Left ⟵

Look again at the diagram showing the classroom lockers.

Complete the following sentences accurately, by choosing the correct phrase or word from the brackets.

Ben's locker is _____ Amy's. (above/underneath)

Jane's locker is _____ Rashmi's. (higher than/next to)

Sajed's locker is _____ Jasmin's. (to the right of/lower than)

Amy's locker is in the _____ . (top row/bottom row)

Rashmi's locker is _____ Robert's. (under/to the left of)

Mark's locker is _____ Rachel's. (lower than/above)

Rosie's locker is _____ Paul's. (below/to the right of)

Josef's locker is _____ Marie's. (higher than/below)

Jane's locker is _____ Rachel's. (above/next to)

Alison's locker is _____ Amy's. (above/to the left of)

Add-on
Using the locker diagram, make up some more sentences of your own.

How to Dazzle at Beginning Mapskills
8

© Vivienne Horobin
This page may be photocopied for use by the purchasing institution only.

In the classroom - plan

FRONT OF CLASSROOM

Teacher

Jane	Humza	Rashid	Susan	Anna

Sally	Rachel	James	David	Ian

Oscar	Martin	Marco	Lucy	Kirsty

John	Alan	Emma	Nicola	Mary

Joanna	Peter	Colin	Michael	Douglas

BACK OF CLASSROOM

In the classroom

Look at the plan of the classroom, which shows a class of children <u>facing</u> the teacher.

Answer these questions:

Who is sitting in front of Ian? _____

Who is sitting to the left of Nicola? _____

Who is sitting behind Humza? _____

Who is sitting directly opposite the teacher? _____

Who is sitting on Colin's right? _____

Who is Alan sitting between? _____ and _____

How many boys are there in the row behind Mary? _____

Who is facing Rashid?_____

Who is sitting next to Kirsty? _____

Who is sitting in the middle of the back row? _____

Look at the classroom plan again.

Word box left front right back behind between middle opposite	**Use the words in the word box to complete each sentence correctly. Don't use the same word twice!**
	James is sitting in _____ of Marco.
	Nicola sits to the _____of Mary.
	Rashid is sitting in the _____ of the front row.
	Lucy sits _____ David.
	The teacher sits _____ Rashid.
	Peter is sitting _____ Colin and Joanna.
	Rachel sits on the _____ of Sally.
	Douglas sits in the _____ row.

Add-on
If you find it hard to remember left and right, find a way to help yourself.
For example, do you always write with your right hand? Do you always wear a watch
on your left wrist? If you have a mark or scar on one hand – remember which one.

Compass points

The trouble with using directions like right, left, behind, in front, is that it depends on which direction we are facing. In order to get over this difficulty on maps, we use compass points. These allow us to give clear directions, as north is always north whichever direction we are facing. So, if we use compass points, we are less likely to make a mistake and we can usually be more accurate.

There are four main compass points:

NORTH   SOUTH   EAST   WEST

The initial letters are often used instead of words. On nearly all maps, north always points upwards towards the top of the map.

Remember:

There are **four** main compass points

NORTH (N)

SOUTH (S)

EAST (E)

WEST (W)

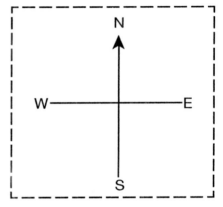

Now cover over the compass diagram in the dotted box.

See if you can label the four main compass points on the diagram below. One compass point has been put in already to help you.

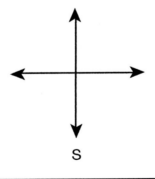

S

Add-on

To help you learn where west and east go, remember that the two letters
W and E make a word across the compass – WE.

Compass practice 1

A diagram showing compass points is called a 'compass rose'. **See if you can label the four main compass points on each of the diagrams on this page.**
Choose from:

  North (N)   West (W)   East (E)   South (S)

On each rose, one compass point has been put in already to help you. Cover over the compass roses you are not working on.

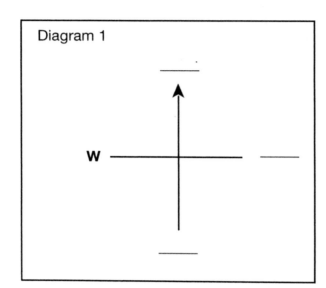

Diagram 1

W

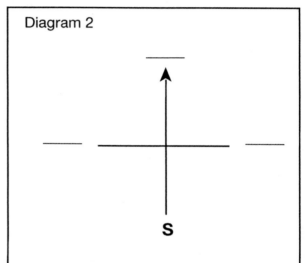

Diagram 2

S

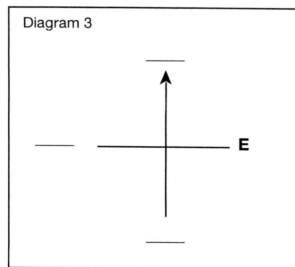

Diagram 3

E

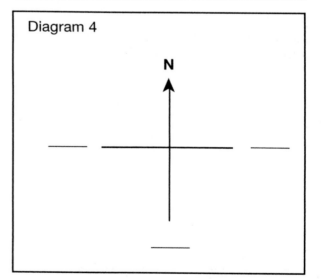

Diagram 4

N

Add-on

Do this with a friend. Draw four more roses like those on this page.
Write one correct compass point on each rose and then swap the rose
with your friend and fill in the other compass points.

Compass practice 2

Colour the circles at each of the four compass points in Diagram 1:

North – red   South – blue   East – yellow   West – green

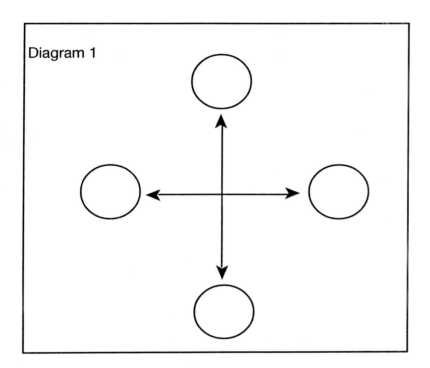

Diagram 1

Hint
Remember, two of the letters make a small word across the compass.

Now, without any help, try to fill in the four compass points on Diagrams 2 and 3.

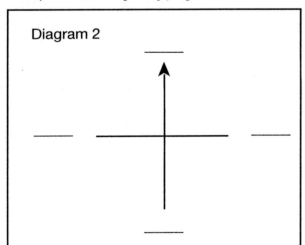

Diagram 2

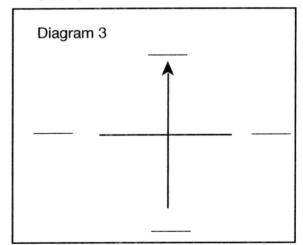

Diagram 3

Add-on
Learn the following phrase to help you remember the order of the compass points – Naughty Elephants Squirt Water. Read round clockwise from the top.

Town route

Martley

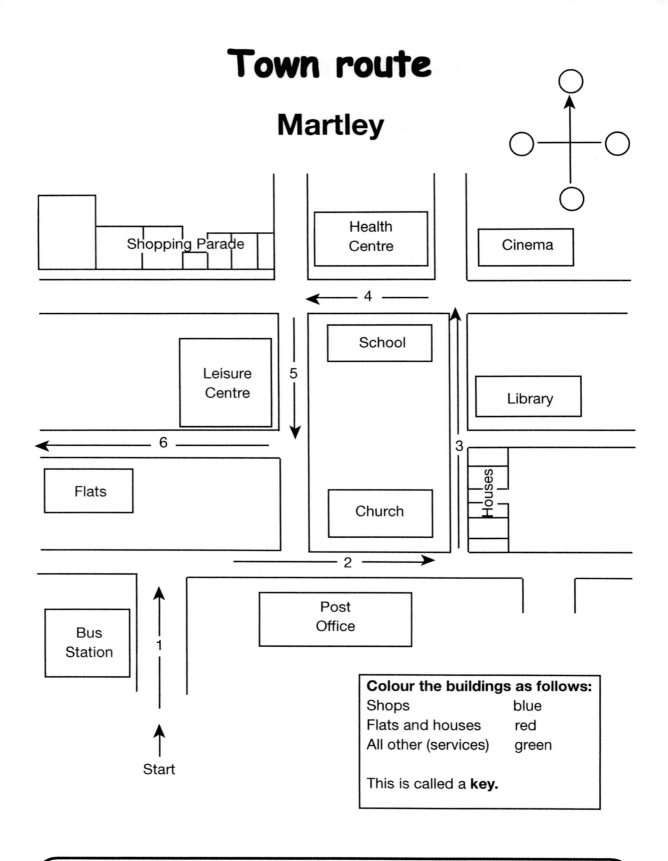

Colour the buildings as follows:

Shops	blue
Flats and houses	red
All other (services)	green

This is called a **key**.

Add-on
Write the correct compass points in the circles of the compass rose
at the top of the page.

Route round Martley

Using the map of Martley, cross out the incorrect word in the brackets in each case to describe the route around the town correctly. Start at 1.

1. I walked (north/south), passing the bus station on my (right/left).

2. At the end of the road, I turned (right/left). As I walked (eastwards/westwards), I saw, first, the post office on my (left/right) and then a church on my (left/right).

3. Just past the church, I turned (left/right) to walk (southwards/northwards). After passing a road junction on my (left/right), I noticed the library to the (left/right).

4. When I reached the junction at the end of the road, I turned (right/left), passing a school on my (right/left). I continued (westwards/eastwards) as far as the crossroads.

5. At the crossroads I turned (left/right), keeping the leisure centre on my (left/right).

6. When I reached the first road junction, just (before/after) the leisure centre, I turned (right/left). The (large/small) building of the leisure centre was still to my (left/right) as I walked (eastwards/westwards). As I reached the end of the road I passed a block of flats on my (left/right).

Add-on
See if you can describe some simple routes round your school. Use words like left, right, straight on, and mention some of the places you pass on the way. With a friend, describe how you would get from your classroom to:
a) the main entrance   b) the dining room   c) the Head's office.
Choose another place to visit and see if you can write the route down.

Car parks in Banford

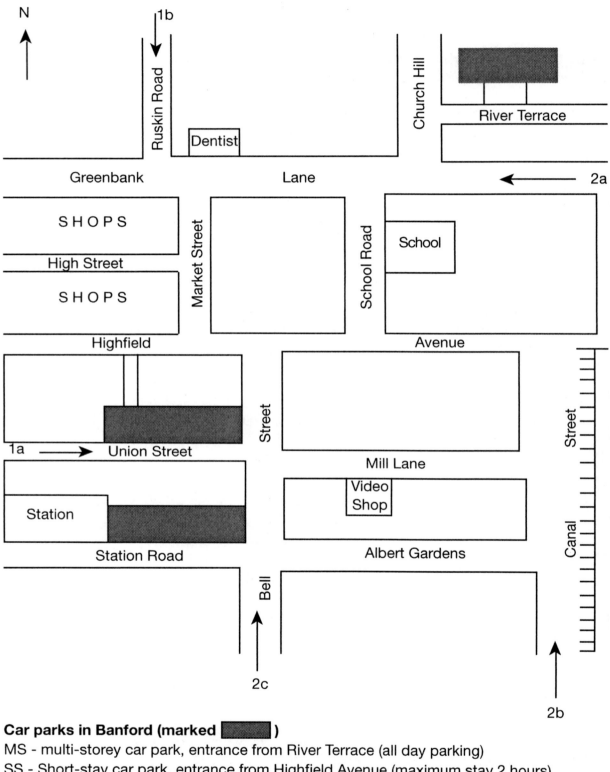

Car parks in Banford (marked ▨)

MS - multi-storey car park, entrance from River Terrace (all day parking)

SS - Short-stay car park, entrance from Highfield Avenue (maximum stay 2 hours)

Station parking - entrance from Station Road (maximum stay 45 minutes)

On street parking in Canal Street (maximum stay 30 minutes) marked └┴┴┴┴┘

Parking in Banford

Look at the map showing the different areas of parking in Banford. Check how long you are allowed to stay in each car park.

Sally and Mr Murray need to park in Banford for different reasons. Read about each one carefully. Decide which car park is the best one for them to use. Describe the route they must take to reach the car park chosen, using the **names of the roads** and the words **left** and **right** to make your explanations clear.

1a. Sally comes into the town on Union Street. She works all day in one of the shops in High Street.

Car park chosen: _____

....

....

....

....

....

....

1b. Mr Murray enters the town using Ruskin Road. He wants to change his video and thinks it should take about 20 minutes.

Car park chosen: _____

....

....

....

....

More routes in Banford

2a. John wants a new pair of trainers.
His mother drives into Banford along Greenbank Lane
and thinks it will only take an hour to find some trainers
John likes.

Car park chosen: _____

....

....

....

....

2b. Jane is going with her father to collect her grandmother
from the Station. They come into Banford along
Canal Street.

Car park chosen: _____

....

....

....

....

2c. Mrs Scott is taking Emily to the dentist and she is usually
there for about 30 minutes. Mrs Scott drives into Banford
along Bell Street.

Car park chosen: _____

....

....

....

....

More compass points

Between each of the four main compass points, we can add four more points to give even greater accuracy. These four extra points are:

NORTHWEST (NW) - between North and West

NORTHEAST (NE) - between North and East

SOUTHWEST (SW) - between South and West

SOUTHEAST (SE) - between South and East

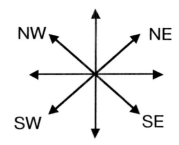

Of course, we can add more and more points but eight points are usually enough for general map reading.

Now check that you understand the letters that we use for the eight compass points. Draw lines to link the names to the correct letters.

NW	North
E	NE
SE	East
West	Southeast
South	W
Northeast	SW
N	S
Southwest	Northwest

Add-on

Test a friend by asking which two points each compass point is between.
Use the list in the box above or just make up your own.
For example: North is between ? and ? Southeast is between ? and ?

Which direction?

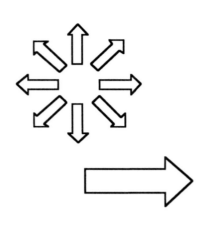

Use the diagram on the left to help you label the direction each arrow points to. Write the answer on the line below each arrow. Colour in each arrow with a different colour. Then colour in the arrows on the compass rose to match your arrows below.

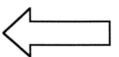

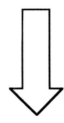

1. ....

2. ....

3. ....

4. ....

5. ....

6. ....

7. ....

8. ....

Add-on

Practise writing all eight compass points around the compass rose to the right of this box. You can colour in the arrows as well if you want to.

Naming eight points

On the diagrams below, label all the compass points. Choose from the following list:

NORTH	SOUTHWEST	NORTHEAST	EAST
WEST	SOUTHEAST	SOUTH	NORTHWEST

Two have been put in already. Use the correct letters in each case.
Cover over the diagrams you are not working on.

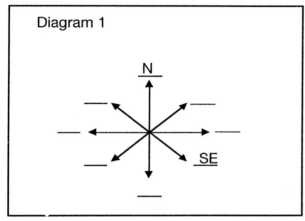

Diagram 1

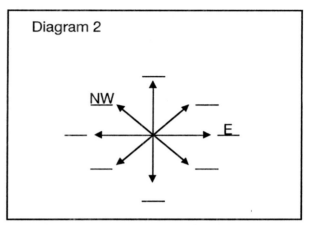

Diagram 2

Now try labelling the compass points on diagrams 3 and 4. This time, only one compass points has been put on each diagram. Again, cover up all the diagrams you are not working on.

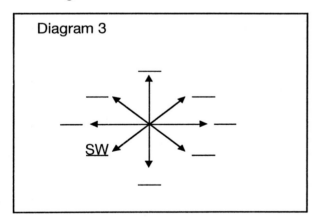

Diagram 3

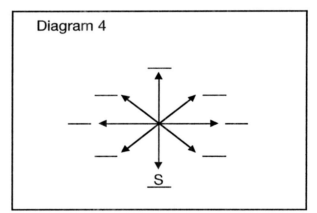

Diagram 4

Add-on
Make a list of some jobs where people might have to use a compass
or know the compass directions.

Eight compass points – going solo

Label the compass points asked for on each of the diagrams below.

Diagram 1
Label: SW, NE, S

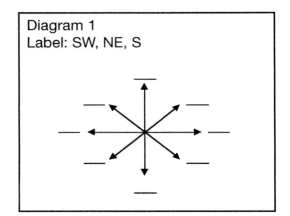

Diagram 2
Label: NE, W, NW

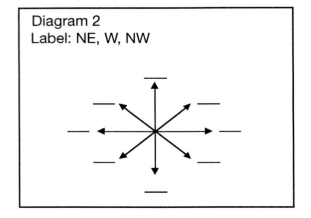

Diagram 3
Label: SE, W, N

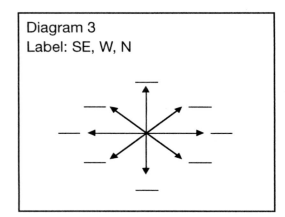

Diagram 4
Label: E, SW. NE

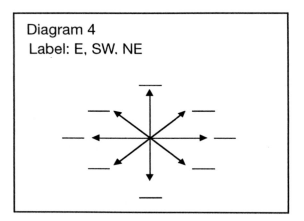

Diagram 5
Label: S, NW, E, SE

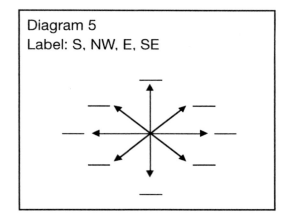

Diagram 6
Label: W, E, NE, SW

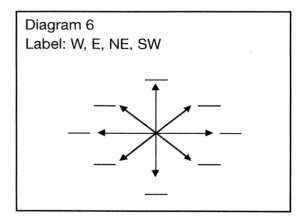

Add-on
Do this in pairs. Draw six compass roses like those in these diagrams and write down one point to be labelled on the first diagram, two points on the second diagram and so on. Swap with your partner and label the points asked for on each compass diagram.

Compass practice – colours and letters

Colour in the squares at the correct compass points as follows:

North   – red
Northwest   – black
South   – green
Southeast   – orange
East   – blue
Northeast   – purple
West   – yellow
Southwest   – brown

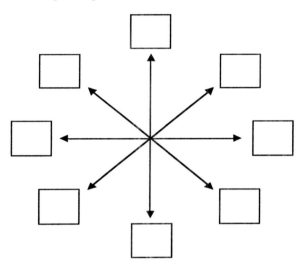

Now try this:

Write the following letters in the correct circles around the compass below.

West - B
East - D
North - E
South - H
Southeast - G
Northeast - F
Southwest - A
Northwest - C

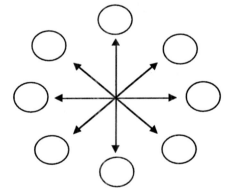

Add-on
In the classroom, decide which wall is north. See if you can give instructions
to a friend which will take them on a route round the room.
Use compass directions and the number of paces they need to take.

More compass practice

Draw the following objects in the correct circles around the compass below:

North   – clock
East   – fork
Northwest – ball
Southeast – pencil
West   – cat
Northeast – bell
Southwest – house
South   – cup

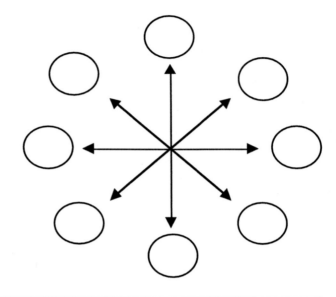

Label the missing compass points in the circles below

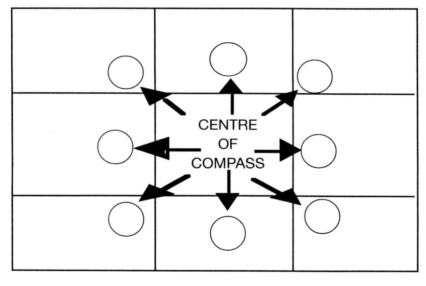

CENTRE
OF
COMPASS

Add-on

Draw a different picture in each square above, except the middle square. Now make up a set of questions for a friend using directions and pictures.
For example: Which direction do you go from the centre to reach the dog?
What is the direction from the dog to the bone?

Alphabet route

Use the alphabet diagram.

Follow the instructions

below moving from

each time to complete

the sentence at the

bottom of the page. The first

one has been done for you.

Q	A	K	◇	B	✦
♡	R	N	X	△	I
M	✦	T	L	V	F
Y	E	□	☺	W	O
G	⬠	H	Z	U	✛
◯	C	D	J	P	S

1. Go north 2 squares, then east 2 squares. (You come to I.)

2. Go west 2 squares, then south 2 squares.

3. Go north 3 squares, then west 2 squares.

4. Go north 2 squares, then west 1 square.

5. Go south 2 squares, then west 1 square.

6. Go east 2 squares.

7. Go north 1 square, then west 1 square.

8. Go west 1 square, then south 1 square.

9. Go east 2 squares, then north 2 squares.

10. Go south 2 squares, then east 2 squares.

___ I ___   ___ ___ ___ ___   ___ ___ ___ ___ ___

Add-on
Make up your own alphabet square and write some directions to send
a secret message to a friend.

Shape maze

See if you can follow this route round the shape maze plan. Colour each shape you come to as instructed. Do **not** go back to the start each time but carry on each time from the last symbol you came to.

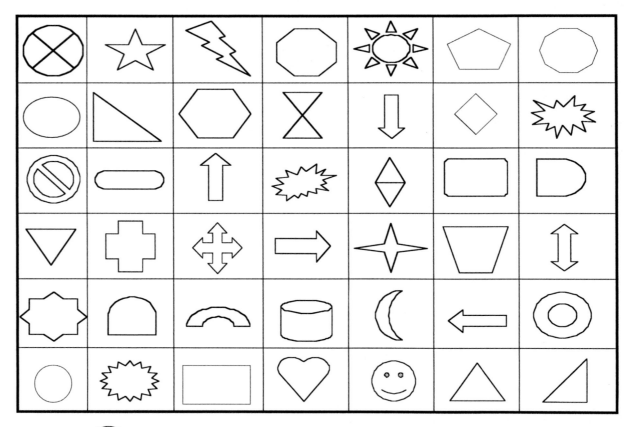

Start at

1. First, go <u>east</u> two squares: colour symbol RED
2. Next go <u>northwest</u> four squares: colour symbol PINK
3. Now go <u>northeast</u> one square: colour symbol BLUE
4. Go <u>south</u> five squares: colour symbol YELLOW
5. Go <u>west</u> one square: colour symbol ORANGE
6. Now go <u>north</u> three squares: colour symbol GREEN
7. Go <u>southeast</u> three squares: colour symbol BROWN
8. Go <u>north</u> five squares: colour symbol PURPLE
9. Finally, go <u>southwest</u> five squares: colour symbol BLACK

Add-on

Name the symbols you have coloured:

1. a red...................................   2. a pink...................................   3. a blue...................................
4. a yellow..............................   5. an orange............................   6. a green................................
7. a brown..............................   8. a purple..............................   9. a black................................

Know your shapes

Colour in the shapes around the compass, following the instructions given.

triangle   –   yellow
hexagon   –   purple
square   –   pink
octagon   –   brown
circle   –   blue
oval   –   orange
diamond   –   red
pentagon –   green

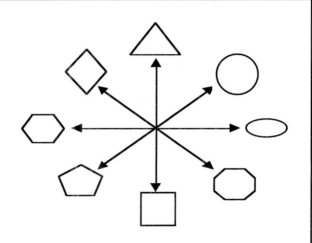

Now try this, using the diagram above.

Read each statement and answer *true* or *false*. The first one has been done for you.

1. To the north is a red diamond.   False

2. To the west is a purple hexagon.   _____

3. There is a pink circle to the south.   _____

4. There is an orange octagon to the southeast.   _____

5. To the northwest is a red diamond.   _____

6. There is a yellow triangle to the north.   _____

7. To the northeast is a blue pentagon.   _____

8. There is a brown octagon to the southeast.   _____

9. The pink square is to the west.   _____

10. There is a green pentagon to the southwest.   _____

Add-on
Make up some more sentences, some true and some false. Give
them to a friend for them to answer true or false.

Wordsearch

See if you can find the names of all eight compass points in the grid. Also, look for some of the words we have used to show position and direction (in the box below). You can go up, down, across, backwards and diagonally.

left	above	under	right	opposite	bottom
lower	next to	top	facing	higher	below
middle	front	back	near	behind	between

N	Q	E	T	I	S	O	P	P	O	B	E	W	M
V	O	D	H	H	E	M	E	X	O	L	O	A	O
N	N	R	G	S	J	Z	H	U	N	L	A	E	T
E	E	S	T	R	O	R	T	H	E	S	E	S	T
E	C	X	L	H	I	T	R	B	A	K	A	A	O
W	I	E	T	G	W	V	O	L	R	E	U	O	B
T	E	W	H	T	Y	E	N	R	H	S	W	K	M
E	A	T	B	W	O	L	S	T	U	O	C	D	J
B	T	S	E	W	S	T	R	T	E	A	S	T	E
R	E	H	G	I	H	O	U	O	B	W	S	N	P
W	E	A	P	X	N	T	U	S	T	U	O	O	U
W	T	N	B	D	I	G	O	T	P	B	U	R	N
E	F	T	E	N	N	U	U	U	H	T	T	F	D
T	E	O	U	I	T	E	T	F	T	E	H	S	E
S	L	P	C	H	Y	V	A	E	O	H	A	C	R
V	X	A	W	E	R	O	P	O	U	T	E	S	O
C	F	E	U	B	I	B	M	I	D	D	L	E	T
U	S	H	T	N	A	A	O	Z	H	P	L	N	S
T	S	A	G	N	H	Q	R	E	W	O	L	E	D

Check what you know

Complete the following passage, using the words in the box below to fill in the gaps.

south	left	east	top	southwest
compass	northwest	right	four	maps

When we are telling people where things are, we use words like left, right and

behind. This way ⟵ is _____

and this way ⟶ is _____ .

However, when looking at _____ we use _____ points rather than

words.

There are _____ main compass points. These are north, _____,

west and _____. North always points towards the _____ of a map.

For greater accuracy, we can add in four more points – southeast, _____,

northeast and _____ .

Add-on

From memory, label the eight compass
points on the diagram below.

Places in the town

Label the compass points on the compass rose diagram.

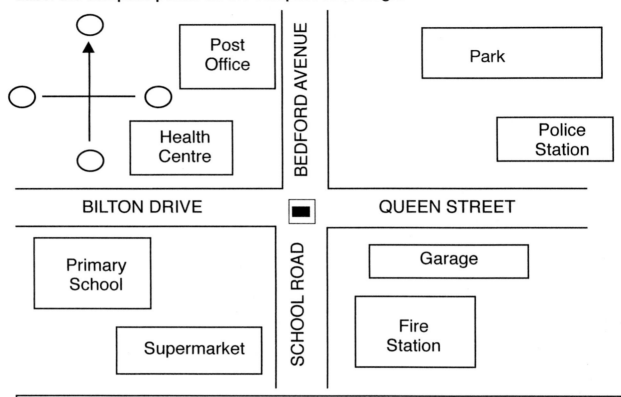

Use the town map above to complete the following sentences correctly by crossing out the incorrect word in the brackets each time. The town centre is at ■ .

1. The Garage is on the (south/north) side of Queen Street.

2. The Primary School is on the (west/east) side of the Garage.

3. The Health Centre is in the (western/southern) part of the town.

4. The Post Office is (west/north) of Bilton Drive.

5. The Fire Station is (east/west) of the supermarket.

6. The Police Station is (northwest/southeast) of the Post Office.

7. The Health Centre is (southwest/northeast) of the Park.

8. School Road runs (south/north) from the Town Centre.

Add-on
See if you can draw some small pictures or **symbols** for the eight places on the map above. They should make it easy to know what the building is.

Land use maps

A land use map is a map that shows how different parts of an area are used. In the country, a land use map might show different types of vegetation (plants), such as forest, marsh or grass, but in a town the map would show which areas were houses, which shops, which offices and so on.

In a town, the main uses can be simply divided into:
- shops
- offices
- residential (housing)
- services
- entertainment

Hint
You probably have no difficulty in deciding which buildings are used as shops, offices, or for housing, but it may be more difficult to decide which are services or entertainment. Generally, a service is something which a trained or skilled person does for you. For example, a service which you might need occasionally could be a doctor. Entertainment is usually something you use to enjoy yourself such as a swimming pool or a cafe.

Colour the small box beside each land use according to the following guide.
This is called a **key** .

shops – red ☐   services – yellow ☐   offices – green ☐

entertainment – brown ☐   residential – blue ☐

Now see if you can decide which land use each of the following buildings have. Using the same key you have made above, colour the box beside each building to match the general land use you think is correct; for example, greengrocer (a shop) = red.

butcher ☐	church ☐	restaurant ☐	dentist ☐
cobbler ☐	flats ☐	supermarket ☐	bank ☐
house ☐	bakery ☐	fire station ☐	council offices ☐

Add-on
Write down a different type of building on the line by each of the boxes below and then swap with a friend and see if you can colour each box with the correct land use.
Use the same key as you did in the box above.

1......................... ☐   2......................... ☐   3......................... ☐

4......................... ☐   5......................... ☐   6......................... ☐

Sorting land use into categories

Label the compass points on the compass rose. Colour in the different land uses as shown in the box and complete the key at the bottom of the page.

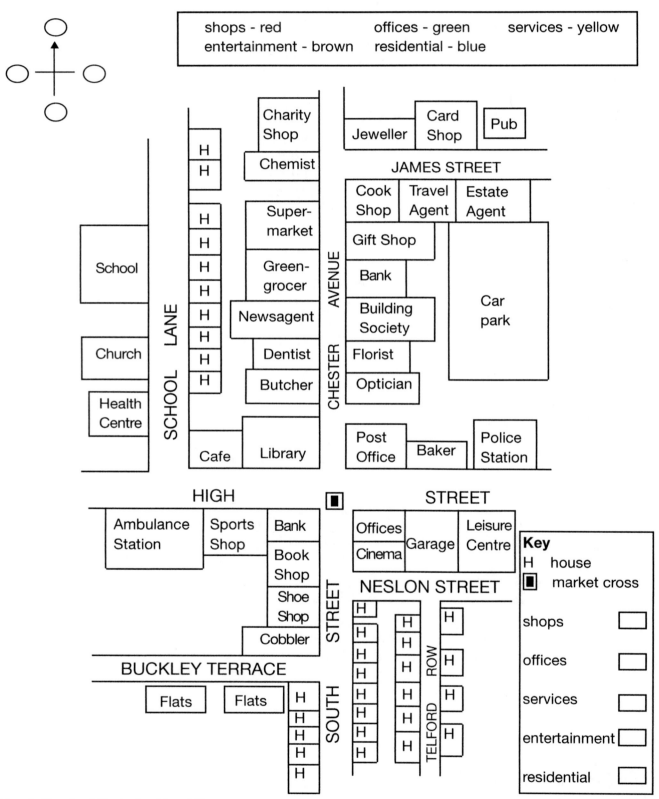

shops - red   offices - green   services - yellow

entertainment - brown   residential - blue

Land use in a town

Look at the map you have coloured on the last page. Now see if you can answer the questions in the box.

In the space given, write true or false to each of the following statements:

1. The newsagent is opposite the building society.   _____

2. The baker is on the south side of South Street.   _____

3. The butcher is north of the cobbler.   _____

4. The High Street runs from west to east.   _____

5. The police station is east of the leisure centre.   _____

6. The flats are northeast of the baker.   _____

7. The church is southeast of the cinema.   _____

8. The Library faces the Post Office.   _____

9. The ambulance station is southwest of the florist.   _____

10. Most of the houses are in the southeast part of the town.   _____

Make your own map by adding names to the roads and labelling the buildings or areas shown with your choice of land use. Add compass directions and a key.

KEY

Add-on

Make up five questions about your map and give them to a friend for them to answer.

Leisure centre

Below is a plan of a leisure centre. Look at it carefully.

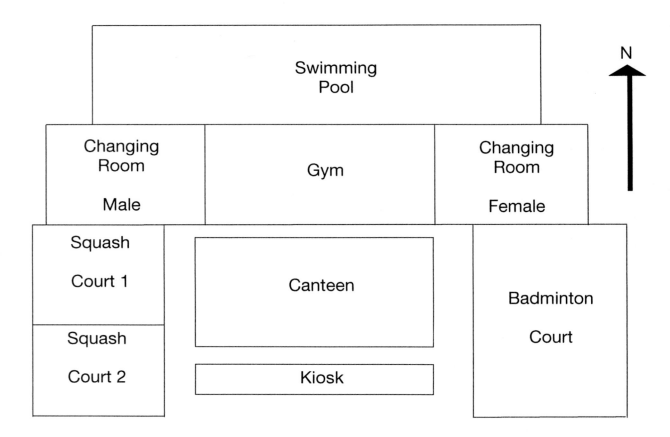

Look at the map of the leisure centre and then cross out the incorrect word in the brackets in each of the statements below.

1. The canteen is (west/east) of the squash courts.
2. The gym is (north/south) of the canteen.
3. The badminton court is (southeast/northwest) of the gym.
4. The female changing room is to the (northwest/northeast) of the canteen.
5. The kiosk is to the (southwest/southeast) of squash court 1.
6. The badminton court is (east/west/north/south) of the canteen.
7. The kiosk is (south/north) of the canteen and (west/east) of squash court 2.

Add-on
Ask for a large sheet of paper. With a partner, design your ideal leisure centre.
Be as imaginative as you can, and include all the sports you would like
as well as any extra facilities you think might be wanted such as
physiotherapist, fitness advisor, and so on.

Where do people work?

You have now seen some maps showing various buildings you are likely to see in a town. Look at the rings at the bottom of the page which show some of the people who work in a town. Cut around dotted lines and stick each name in the space underneath the building where you think they work.

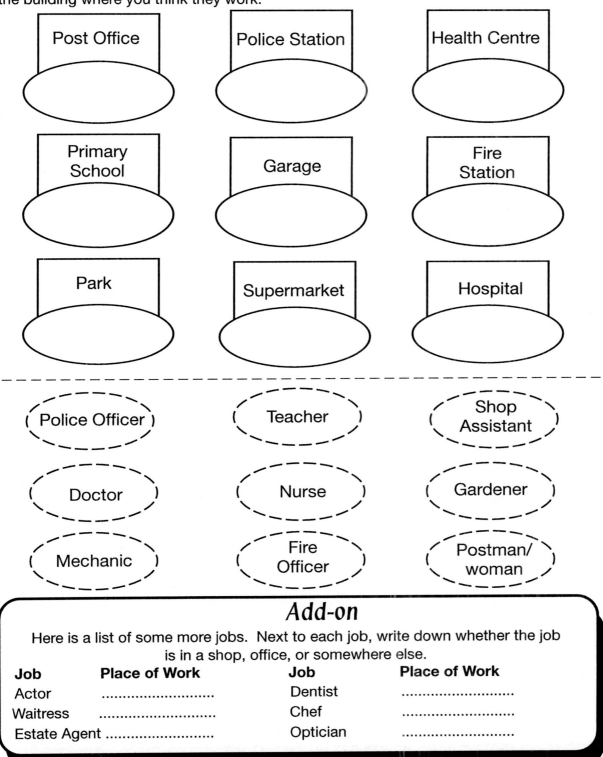

Add-on

Here is a list of some more jobs. Next to each job, write down whether the job is in a shop, office, or somewhere else.

Job	Place of Work	Job	Place of Work
Actor	....	Dentist	....
Waitress	....	Chef	....
Estate Agent	....	Optician	....

Who does what?

Try to link each person with the phrase that describes them best.

May give you medicine to make you better	Farmer
Might bring you a parcel	Gardener
Wears a bright yellow helmet	Teacher
Mends the car when it breaks down	Musician
Might use a spade at work	Shop Assistant
Should be able to give you the right change	Pilot
Helps you learn at school	Fire Officer
Might sing or play an instrument	Cobbler
Helps you cross the road	Postman/woman
Flies an aeroplane	Mechanic
Sells meat in his shop	Author
Sometimes drives a tractor	Doctor
Writes books	Butcher
Mends shoes	Lollipop lady/man

Recording wind direction

Wind direction is recorded using a wind rose. The direction shown is the direction the wind has come from as this gives us some idea of how warm or cold the wind might be. For example, we would expect a northerly wind to be colder than a wind from the south. A wind rose shows wind direction clearly as, at a glance, you can see how often the wind comes from any particular direction.

In Britain, general characteristics of the wind can be summarised as:

North – cold
East – dry; cold in winter, warm in summer
South – warm
West – moist; warm in winter, cool in summer

The wind rose below shows the wind direction for the month of September.

Each small rectangle represents one day.

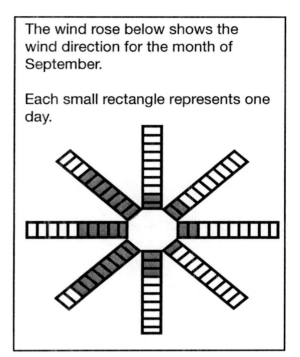

Look carefully at the wind rose for September and then answer these questions.

1. How many days did the wind blow from the east? _____

2. From which direction does the wind blow most often? _____

3. Does the wind blow more from the west or from the north? _____

4. Is there more likely to be a wind from the southwest or northeast? _____

5. From which direction did the wind blow for three days? _____

Add-on

Use the wind rose at the right of this box and plot the wind direction every day for one week.

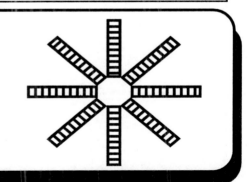

Wind rose for June

Wind data for June - direction of the wind (where it has come from)

June 1st	Southwest	June 11th	North	June 21st	Southwest
June 2nd	West	June 12th	North	June 22nd	Southwest
June 3rd	West	June 13th	Northeast	June 23rd	South
June 4th	Northwest	June 14th	Southwest	June 24th	South
June 5th	North	June 15th	Southwest	June 25th	West
June 6th	Northwest	June 16th	Southwest	June 26th	Northwest
June 7th	Northwest	June 17th	South	June 27th	West
June 8th	Southwest	June 18th	West	June 28th	Southwest
June 9th	Southwest	June 19th	Northwest	June 29th	South
June 10th	Northwest	June 20th	West	June 30th	Southeast

Shade in the wind rose in the following way. Shade in one small section for each day.

Make sure you choose the 'arm' which points in the direction the wind has come from.

Colour in the section nearest to the centre first and gradually move outwards.

Wind rose

N

Add-on

From which direction does the wind blow most often? _____

The British Isles

Wherever you live on the map below, you live in the British Isles, which is the name given to the two big islands shown, together with all the smaller islands around them. However, different names are given to different parts of the British Isles, depending on which countries are included. These names are:

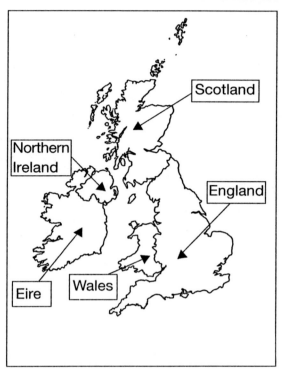

The United Kingdom
Great Britain
Republic of Ireland
(sometimes called **Eire**)
The British Isles
Ireland

> If you look at the bottom of the page, you will see what is meant by each of these names.

> How many countries are in each of the following?
>
> Great Britain   ....
> Ireland   ....
> United Kingdom   ....
> British Isles   ....

> On the map above, colour each country as given below.
>
> | | |
> |---|---|
> | England | red |
> | Northern Ireland | yellow |
> | Republic of Ireland (Eire) | green |
> | Scotland | blue |
> | Wales | purple |

> Put the countries of the British Isles in alphabetical order.
>
> Scotland   ....
> Wales   ....
> England   ....
> Northern Ireland   ....
> Eire   ....

The British Isles	**Great Britian**	**United Kingdom**	**Republic of Ireland**
England	England	England	Republic of Ireland
Northern Ireland	Scotland	Northern Ireland	
Republic of Ireland	Wales	Scotland	**Ireland**
Scotland		Wales	Northern Ireland
Wales			Republic of Ireland

Countries of the British Isles

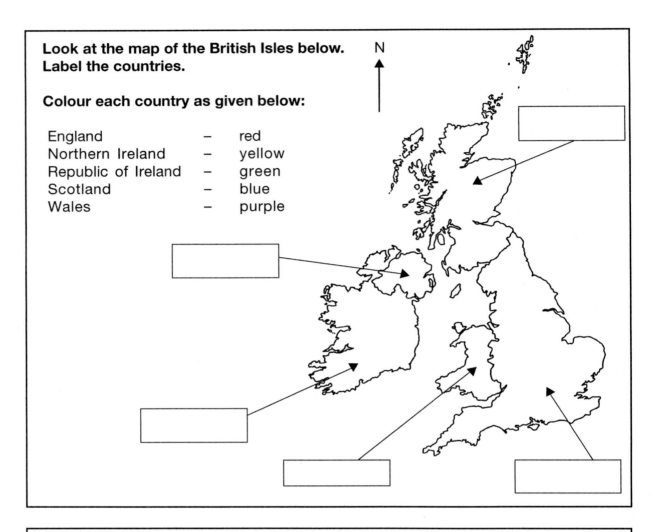

**Look at the map of the British Isles below.
Label the countries.**

Colour each country as given below:

England   –   red
Northern Ireland   –   yellow
Republic of Ireland –   green
Scotland   –   blue
Wales   –   purple

N

Answer true or false to each of the following statements:

1. Northern Ireland is sometimes called Eire.   _____

2. There are three countries in the United Kingdom.   _____

3. Great Britain is larger than Ireland.   _____

4. Ireland is east of Great Britain.   _____

5. Ireland is closer to Scotland than to Wales.   _____

6. The largest country in the British Isles is Scotland. _____

Add-on

Make a list of all the countries in the British Isles. Using your judgment,
write them in size order with the largest one first and the smallest one last.

Seas around the British Isles

Label the countries of the British Isles in the boxes shown.

See if you can name the seas around the British Isles using the clues below.
Write the names on the lines given.

❖ The North Sea is to the east of Scotland and England.
❖ The Irish Sea is between Ireland and Great Britain.
❖ The English Channel is to the south of England.
❖ The Atlantic Ocean is to the west of the British Isles.

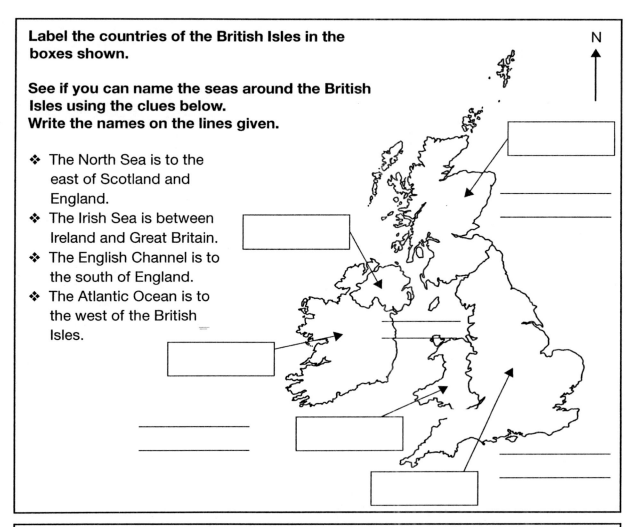

For each sentence, cross out the incorrect word or phrase in the brackets.

1. The North Sea is (east/west) of Great Britain.

2. Scotland is (west/east) of the North Sea.

3. The Irish Sea is to the (east/north) of Ireland.

4. The Atlantic Ocean is (west/east) of the United Kingdom.

5. England is (north/south) of the English Channel.

6. The Irish Sea is to the west of (Wales/Eire).

Add-on
Use an atlas to find out which other countries have a coastline with
a) the North Sea   b) the Atlantic Ocean   c) the English Channel

Capital cities of the British Isles

On this map, lines have been drawn to divide the British Isles into four quarters or sectors. Using the information below, label the five capital cities on the map marked ●.

N ↑

County	Capital city
England	London
Northern Ireland	Belfast
Republic of Ireland	Dublin
Scotland	Edinburgh
Wales	Cardiff

Imagine that the centre of a compass is placed where the two lines through the British Isles cross. Now write true or false by each statement below.

1. London is in the western half of Britain. _____

2. Belfast is southwest of Edinburgh. _____

3. Cardiff is to the west of London. _____

4. Edinburgh is the northeast sector of the British Isles. _____

5. Dublin is in the northwest part of the British Isles. _____

Add-on
Write down which capital city in Britain is the furthest: a) north _____
b) south _____   c) west _____   d) east _____

The British Isles - revision

Use the words in the box to fill the gaps in the sentences below. You can use each word only once.

Edinburgh	Ireland	three	North Sea
English Channel	between	London	Atlantic Ocean
Belfast	two	four	England

1. The Irish Sea lies _____ Ireland and Great Britain.

2. There are _____ countries in Great Britain.

3. The two capital cities in Ireland are _____ and Dublin.

4. The _____ is the sea to the south of England.

5. The capital city of Scotland is _____ .

6. _____ is joined to Wales and Scotland.

7. There are _____ countries in the United Kingdom.

8. The capital city of the United Kingdom is _____.

9. The _____ is the name of the sea to the west of Ireland.

10. There are _____ countries in Ireland.

11. The sea to the east of Great Britain is called the _____.

12. The large island to the west of Great Britain is called _____ .

Answer the following questions:

1. In which country is Cardiff? _____

2. Is the United Kingdom smaller or larger than Great Britain? _____

3. How many countries are there in the British Isles? _____

4. Name the two capital cities in Ireland. _____

5. Which country in the British Isles is furthest east? _____

6. Name the countries in Great Britain. _____

7. What is the most northern country of the British Isles? _____

8. Name the sea between Ireland and Great Britain. _____

9. What is the smallest country in Great Britain? _____

10. What is another name for the Republic of Ireland? _____

Where I live

Use an atlas to help you and mark where you live on the map below with a dot ●. Write the name of your town or village clearly next to the dot.

Write the names of the capital cities in the boxes and the names of the seas and oceans on the lines.

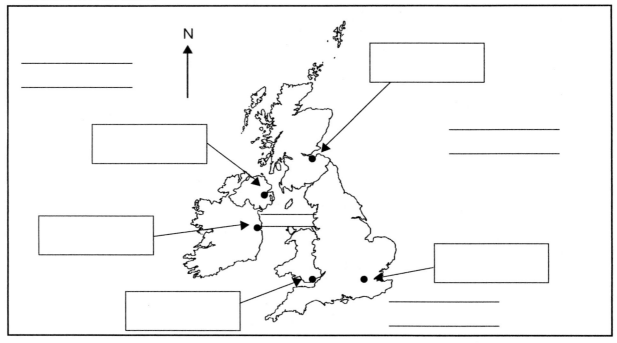

Read each of the statements below and then cross out the incorrect word in the brackets in each statement. Look at the map above to help you.

1. I live (north/south) of London.

2. I live (north/south) of Edinburgh.

3. I live (east/west) of Cardiff.

4. I live in (Great Britain/Ireland/on a smaller island).

5. I live in (Wales/England/Scotland/Northern Ireland/Eire).

6. I live (east/west) of the Irish Sea.

Add-on
See if you can write one sentence which describes where you live, using some ideas from the box above, and the names of capital cities and seas if necessary.

European countries

Cut out the eight European countries at the bottom of the page and stick them at the compass points instructed.

Denmark	west
France	east
Norway	north
Italy	south
United Kingdom	southwest
Germany	northwest
Greece	northeast
Spain	southeast

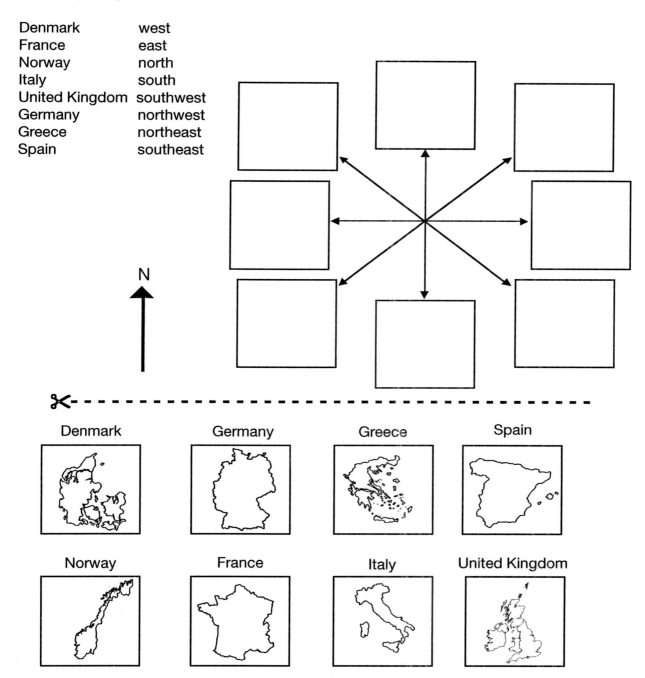

✂- -

Denmark   Germany   Greece   Spain

Norway   France   Italy   United Kingdom

Add-on
Find a map which shows the countries of Europe clearly. Imagine you live in Switzerland. Write down the countries above as a list and next to each country, write down the direction you would have to go to get there from Switzerland.

Anna's holidays

Anna lives in Germany but spends her holidays travelling in Europe. So far, she has visited eight countries. See if you can name each one. Write the name of the country on the line above the each map. Use an atlas if you need to.

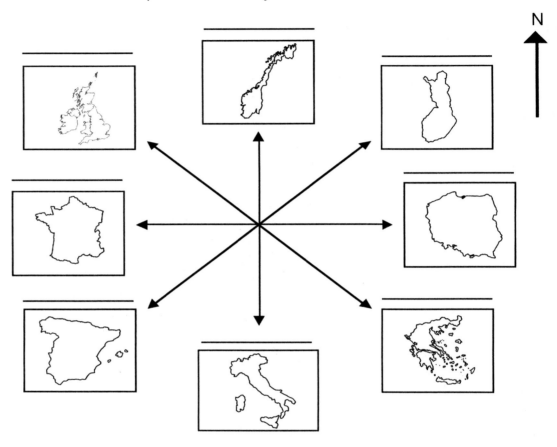

Look at the compass diagram above and complete the
sentences below by writing in the missing country or direction.

1. Anna travelled _____ to Norway.

2. Anna travelled southeast to _____ .

3. Anna travelled south to _____ .

4. Anna travelled _____ to Poland.

5. Anna travelled _____ to Spain.

The world – continents and hemispheres

The map below shows the world divided into hemispheres, or 'half spheres'. The east and west hemispheres are divided by the Prime Meridian and the north and south hemispheres are divided by the equator.

Continents
North America
Africa
Oceania
South America
Europe
Antarctica
Asia

Use an atlas to label the continents on the world map below.

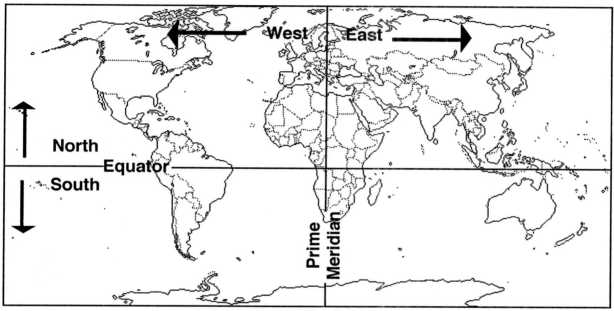

Read each statement below and write <u>true</u> or <u>false</u> in the space given.

1. North America is entirely in the northern hemisphere. _____

2. Oceania is southeast of Europe. _____

3. The equator passes through only two continents. _____

4. The Prime Meridian passes through Europe and Africa. _____

5. On this map Asia lies to the west of Africa. _____

6. Europe is entirely in the eastern hemisphere. _____

7. North America is west of the Prime Meridian. _____

8. Europe is entirely in the northern hemisphere. _____

9. Asia is joined to Africa and Europe. _____

10. South America is in the eastern hemisphere. _____

The world - revision

Cross out the incorrect word or phrase in each sentence below.

1. There are (six/seven) continents.

2. (Antarctica/South America) is the southernmost continent.

3. The equator runs through (Africa/Europe).

4. Africa is (south/north) of Europe.

5. The Prime Meridian runs from (north to south/east to west).

6. The equator runs through (South America/North America).

7. Most of the world's land is in the (southern/northern) hemisphere.

8. The Prime Meridian runs through (two/three) continents.

9. Asia is entirely in the (western/eastern) hemisphere.

10. Asia is (smaller/larger) than South America.

Write down the names of the continents the equator crosses.

_____

Write down the names of the continents the Prime Meridian crosses.

_____

Write down the name of all the continents crossed by both the Prime Meridian and

the equator._____

Complete the sentences below correctly, using the words in the word box.

Asia is _____ than South America. There are only _____

continents entirely in the northern hemisphere. The equator passes

through _____ continents. Europe is _____ than

Africa. The _____ divides the northern and southern

hemispheres. There are _____continents altogether.

Word box
equator
seven
three
two
larger
smaller

Add-on

How many countries does the equator pass through?   _____
How many countries does the Prime Meridian pass through? _____

Answers

Where are the lockers   page 8
true, false, false, true, false, true, false, true, false, true
underneath, next to, lower than, top row, under, above, to the right of, higher than, above, to the left of

In the classroom   page 10
Anna, Emma, Rachel, Rashid, Michael, John and Emma, 4, the teacher, Lucy, Colin
front, left, middle, behind, opposite, between, right, back

Route around Martley   page 15
1. north, left
2. right, eastwards, right, left
3. left, northwards, right, right
4. left, left, westwards
5. left, right
6. after, right, large, right, westwards, left

Alphabet route   page 25
I CAN DO THIS

Shape maze   page 26
1. triangle
2. hexagon
3. octagon
4. heart
5. rectangle
6. arrow
7. triangle
8. pentagon
9. circle

Know your shapes   page 27
true, false, false, true, true, false, true, false, true

Wordsearch   page 28

Places in town   page 30
1. south
2. west
3. western
4. north
5. east
6. southeast
7. southwest
8. south

Land use in a town   page 33
true, false, true, true, false, false, false, true, true, true

Leisure centre   page 34
1. east
2. north
3. southeast
4. northeast
5. southeast
6. east
7. south, east

Countries of the British Isles   page 40
false, false, true, false, true, false

Seas around the British Isles   page 41
1. east
2. west
3. east
4. west
5. north
6. Wales

Answers

Capital cities of the British Isles
page 42
false, true, true, false, false

The British Isles – revision page 43
1. between	2. three
3. Belfast	4. English Channel
5. Edinburgh	6. England
7. four	8. London
9. Atlantic Ocean	10. two
11. North Sea	12. Ireland

1. Wales	2. larger
3. five	4. Dublin, Belfast
5. England	
6. England, Scotland, Wales	
7. Scotland	8. Irish Sea
9. Wales	10. Eire

Anna's holidays   page 46
1. north	2. Greece
3. Italy	4. east
5. southwest	

The world – continents and hemispheres
page 47
true, true, false, true, false, false, true, true, true, false

The world – revision   page 48
1. seven	2. Antarctica
3. Africa	4. south
5. north to south	6. South America
7. northern	8. three
9. eastern	10. larger

South America, Africa and Oceania
Europe, Africa, Antarctica
Africa
larger, two, three, smaller, equator, seven

Also from Brilliant Publications

How to be Brilliant at Recording in Geography

SUE LLOYD

Flexible photocopiable worksheets designed to lead children through a range of geographical skills. Help pupils learn to investigate places and themes, gain knowledge and understanding about places and themes, ask geographical questions, develop the ability to recognize and explain geographical patterns and become aware of how places fit into a wider geographical context using these flexible photocopiable writing frames.

Printed in the United Kingdom
by Lightning Source UK Ltd.
102619UKS00001B/197-230